The Little Book of Shakespeare

HarperCollins*Publishers*

Published by HarperCollins*Publishers* Ltd
77-85 Fulham Palace Road
London W6 8JB
www.**fire**and**water**.com
© selection Kate Mannion and John Mannion
First published 1999
ISBN 000 325 254 X

All quotations taken from the Alexander Text of Shakespeare's works,
published by HarperCollins*Publishers*.

British Library Cataloguing in Publication Data
A catalogue record for this book is available from the British Library.

Printed and bound by Edinburgh Press, UK

Contents

A Note from the Editors

William Shakespeare famously said that music is the food of love. We think that Shakespeare is food for thought. This collection of quotations gives you a chance to taste the power, wit and wisdom of Shakespeare's poems and plays. The ideas in it cover areas of life which are significant for all of us, and are expressed in language that is always striking, effective and memorable.

You can chew on a single quotation all day, or you can browse through whole sections. Whichever you choose, you will find something that will inspire, intrigue or amuse you.

K.M. & J.M.

$\mathcal{L}$et me not to the marriage of true minds

Admit impediments. Love is not love

Which alters when it alteration finds.

Sonnet 116

$\mathcal{L}ove$ a

There's beggary in the love that can be reckon'd.

Antony and Cleopatra 1 i

CHARMIAN *In* each thing give him way;
cross him in nothing.

CLEOPATRA Thou teachest like a fool –
the way to lose him.

Antony and Cleopatra 1 iii

8

*A*ge cannot wither her, nor custom stale
Her infinite variety. Other women cloy
The appetites they feed, but she makes
    hungry
Where most she satisfies.

Antony and Cleopatra 2 ii

9

If thou rememb'rest not the slightest folly

That ever love did make thee run into,

Thou hast not lov'd.

As You Like It 2 iv

Love a

*M*en have died from time to time, and
worms have eaten them, but not for love

As You Like It 4 i

d Sex

*M*en are April when they woo,

December when they wed: maids are May

when they are maids, but the sky changes

when they are wives.

As You Like It 4 i

Love a

$\mathcal{D}$oubt thou the stars are fire,

Doubt that the sun doth move

Doubt truth to be a liar,

But never doubt I love.

Hamlet 2 ii

*I*s it not strange that desire should so many years outlive performance?

Henry the Fourth – Part Two 2 iv

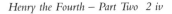

She's beautiful, and therefore to be woo'd;
She is a woman, therefore to be won.

Henry the Sixth – Part One 5 iii

d Sex

But love is blind, and lovers cannot see
The pretty follies that themselves commit.

The Merchant of Venice 2 vi

*T*hings base and vile, holding no quantity,

Love can transpose to form and dignity.

Love looks not with the eyes, but with
the mind;

And therefore is wing'd Cupid painted
blind.

A Midsummer Night's Dream 1 i

nd Sex

The course of true love never did
run smooth.

A Midsummer Night's Dream 1 i

To say the truth, reason and love keep
little company together now-a-days.

A Midsummer Night's Dream 3 i

Love a

*H*ere she comes, curst and sad.

Cupid is a knavish lad,

Thus to make poor females mad.

A Midsummer Night's Dream 3 ii

nd Sex

*H*ow like a winter hath my absence been
From thee, the pleasure of the fleeting year!
What freezings have I felt, what dark
    days seen!
What old December's bareness everywhere!

Sonnet 97

Love a

Friendship is constant in all other things
Save in the office and affairs of love.

Much Ado About Nothing 2 i

$\int$igh no more, ladies, sigh no more!

Men were deceivers ever,

One foot in sea, and one on shore;

To one thing constant never.

Much Ado About Nothing 2 iii

*P*erdition catch my soul,

But I do love thee; and when I love thee
  not,

Chaos is come again.

Othello 3 iii

$\mathcal{B}$ut, soft! what light through yonder
window breaks?
It is the east, and Juliet is the sun.

Romeo and Juliet 2 ii

Love a

*M*y bounty is as boundless as the sea,
My love as deep; the more I give to thee,
The more I have, for both are infinite.

Romeo and Juliet 2 ii

nd Sex

Give me my Romeo; and, when he shall die,
Take him and cut him out in little stars,
And he will make the face of heaven so fine
That all the world will be in love with night
And pay no worship to the garish sun.

Romeo and Juliet 3 ii

Love a

Th' expense of spirit in a waste of shame
Is lust in action.

Sonnet 129

This is the monstruosity in love, lady, that the will is infinite, and the execution confin'd; that the desire is boundless, and the act a slave to limit.

Troilus and Cressida 3 ii

Love

*L*ove sought is good, but given unsought
is better.

Twelfth Night 3 i

*T*hey do not love that do not show
their love.

The Two Gentlemen of Verona 1 ii

*L*ove comforteth like sunshine after rain.

Venus and Adonis

Money

He that wants money, means, and
content, is without three good friends.

As You Like It 3 ii

Money

*N*either a borrower nor a lender be;

For loan oft loses both itself and friend

Hamlet 1 iii

$\mathscr{I}$ can get no remedy against this consumption of the purse: borrowing only lingers and lingers it out, but the disease is incurable.

Henry the Fourth – Part Two 1 ii

Like a poor beggar raileth on the rich.

Well, whiles I am a beggar, I will rail

And say there is no sin but to be rich;

And being rich, my virtue then shall be

To say there is no vice but beggary.

King John 2 i

Money

Fathers that wear rags
Do make their children blind;
But fathers that bear bags
Shall see their children kind.

King Lear 2 iv

Money

Through tatter'd clothes small vices do
appear;
Robes and furr'd gowns hide all.

King Lear 4 vi

If thou art rich, thou'rt poor;

For, like an ass whose back with ingots bows,

Thou bear'st thy heavy riches but a journey,

And Death unloads thee.

Measure for Measure 3 i

Work

To business that we love we rise betime
And go to't with delight.

Antony and Cleopatra 4 iv

Work

I will praise any man that will praise me

Better to leave undone than by our deed
Acquire too high a fame when him we
serve's away.

Antony and Cleopatra 3 i

$\mathcal{I}$f all the year were playing holidays,

To sport would be as tedious as to work;

But when they seldom come, they

    wish'd-for come.

Henry the Fourth – Part One 1 ii

The first thing we do, let's kill all the lawyers.

Henry the Sixth – Part Two 4 ii

Work

Let me have men about me that are fat,

Sleek-headed men, and such as sleep

   o' nights:

Yond Cassius has a lean and hungry look;

He thinks too much. Such men are

   dangerous.

Julius Caesar 1 ii

That sir which serves and seeks for gain,

And follows but for form,

Will pack when it begins to rain

And leave thee in the storm.

King Lear 2 iv

Small have continual plodders ever won,
Save base authority from others' books.

Love's Labours Lost 1 i

Work

He that is well paid is well satisfied

The Merchant of Venice 4 i

Work

O, how full of briers is this working-day world!

As You Like It 1 iii

Reflections *on* *Life*

The web of our life is of a mingled yarn, good and ill together. Our virtues would be proud if our faults whipt them not; and our crimes would despair if they were not cherish'd by our virtues.

All's Well That Ends Well 4 iii

*P*raising what is lost

Makes the remembrance dear.

All's Well That Ends Well 5 iii

Reflectio

The nature of bad news infects the teller.

Antony and Cleopatra 1 ii

All strange and terrible events are
    welcome,
But comforts we despise; our size of sorrow,
Proportion'd to our cause, must be as great
As that which makes it.

Antony and Cleopatra 4 xv

Reflectio

*W*hen I was at home I was in a better place; but travellers must be content.

As You Like It 2 iv

This above all – to thine own self be true,

And it must follow, as the night the day,

Thou canst not then be false to any man.

Hamlet 1 iii

Reflectio

...*b*revity is the soul of wit,

And tediousness the limbs and outward

flourishes.

Hamlet 2 ii

*T*o be, or not to be – that is the question:

Whether 'tis nobler in the mind to suffer

The slings and arrows of outrageous
   fortune

Or to take arms against a sea of troubles,

And by opposing end them?

Hamlet 3 i

Reflectio

...*W*ise men never sit and wail their loss,

but cheerily seek how to redress their

harms.

Henry the Sixth — Part Three 5 iv

s *on Life*

Men at some time are masters of their
    fates:
The fault, dear Brutus, is not in our stars,
But in ourselves, that we are underlings.

Julius Caesar 1 ii

Reflectio

There is a tide in the affairs of men

Which, taken at the flood, leads on

to fortune;

Omitted, all the voyage of their life

Is bound in shallows and in miseries.

Julius Caesar 4 iii

*N*othing can come of nothing.

King Lear 1 i

Reflecti

$\mathcal{O}$, reason not the need! Our basest beggars
Are in the poorest thing superfluous.
Allow not nature more than nature needs,
Man's life is cheap as beast's.

King Lear 2 iv

s on Life

A jest's prosperity lies in the ear
Of him that hears it, never in the tongue
Of him that makes it.

Love's Labours Lost 5 ii

Reflecti

$\mathcal{T}$omorrow, and tomorrow, and tomorrow

Creeps in this petty pace from day to day

To the last syllable of recorded time;

And all our yesterdays have lighted fools

The way to dusty death. Out, out,

brief candle!

Macbeth 5 v

It is a wise father that knows his own child.

The Merchant of Venice 2 ii

Reflectio

The robbed that smiles steals something
from the thief.

Othello 1 iii

67

Things won are done, joy's soul lies in
the doing

Troilus and Cressida 1 ii

Reflectio

...*b*e not afraid of greatness. Some are
born great, some achieve greatness, and
some have greatness thrust upon 'em

Twelfth Night 2 v

Appearance

&

Reality

...*M*eet it is I set it down

That one may smile, and smile, and be

   a villain

Hamlet 1 v

...there is nothing either good or bad, but thinking makes it so.

Hamlet 2 ii

Appearance

Wisdom and goodness to the vile seem
vile;

Filths savour but themselves

King Lear 4 ii

and Reality

The devil can cite Scripture for his purpose.

The Merchant of Venice 1 iii

Appearance

*W*hat's in a name? That which we call a rose
By any other name would smell as sweet.

Romeo and Juliet 2 ii

nd Reality

For sweetest things turn sourest by their
deeds

Lilies that fester smell far worse than weeds.

Sonnet 94

Hopes & Fears

*I*n time we hate that which we often fear.

Antony and Cleopatra 1 iii

$\mathcal{A}$nd these our lives, exempt from public haunt, find tongues in trees, books in the running brooks, sermons in stone, and good in everything.

As You Like It 2 i

Fear no more the heat o' th' sun,

Nor the furious winter's rages.

Thou thy worldly task hast done,

Home art gone and ta'en thy wages.

Cymbeline 4 ii

The time is out of joint. O cursed spite
That ever I was born to set it right!

Hamlet 1 v

*W*hat a piece of work is a man! How noble in reason! how infinite in faculty! in form and moving how express and admirable!

Hamlet 2 ii

*Y*et better thus, and known to be
   contemn'd,
Than still contemn'd and flatter'd. To
   be worst,
The lowest and most dejected thing
   of fortune,
Stands still in esperance, lives not in fear.
The lamentable change is from the best;
The worst returns to laughter.

King Lear 4 i

$\mathcal{I}$ have almost forgot the taste of fears.

The time has been my senses would

   have cool'd

To hear a night-shriek, and my fell of hair

Would at a dismal treatise rouse and stir

As life were in't. I have supp'd full with

   horrors

Macbeth 5 v

Hopes a

True hope is swift and flies with
  swallow's wings;
Kings it makes gods, and meaner
  creatures kings

Richard the Third 5 ii

d Fears

85

...*T*ime will come and take my love away.

This thought is as a death which cannot
   choose

But weep to have, that which it fears to
   lose.

Sonnet 64

Hopes a

*H*ow many goodly creatures are there
    here!
How beauteous mankind is! O brave
    new world
That has such people in't!

The Tempest 5 i

*O*ur doubts are traitors and make us lose

the good we might win, by fearing

to attempt

Measure for Measure 1 iv

Sorrow

*M*y heart is heavy, and mine age is weak;
Grief would have tears, and sorrow bids
  me speak.

All's Well That Ends Well 3 iv

The tears live in an onion that should

water this sorrow.

Antony and Cleopatra 1 ii

Sorrow

When sorrows come, they come not
single spies.
But in battalions!

Hamlet 4 v

Sorrow

*Y*ou have seen

Sunshine and rain at once: her smiles and
    tears

Were like a better way. Those happy smilets

That play'd on her ripe lip seem'd not
    to know

What guests were in her eyes, which
    parted thence

As pearls from diamonds dropp'd. In brief,

Sorrow would be a rarity most belov'd,

If all could so become it.

King Lear 4 iii

*H*ow much better is it to weep at joy

than to joy at weeping!

Much Ado About Nothing 1 i

*W*ell, every one can master a grief but he

that has it.

Much Ado About Nothing 3 ii

He jests at scars that never felt a wound.

Romeo and Juliet 2 ii

Sorrow

Parting is such sweet sorrow,

That I shall say good night till it be

morrow.

Romeo and Juliet 2 ii

Sorrow

*W*hat's gone and what's past help
Should be past grief.

The Winter's Tale 3 ii

Vices & Virtues

*W*ould you have me

False to my nature? Rather say I play

The man I am.

Coriolanus 3 ii

$\mathcal{D}$o not as some ungracious pastors do,

Show me the steep and thorny way

to heaven,

Whiles, like a puff'd and reckless libertine,

Himself the primrose path of dalliance

treads

Hamlet 1 iii

Vices an

*U*se every man after his desert, and who should scape whipping? Use them after your own honour and dignity. The less they deserve: the more merit is in your bounty.

Hamlet 2 ii

Virtues

Give me that man

That is not passion's slave, and I will
  wear him

In my heart's core, ay, in my heart of
  hearts.

Hamlet 3 ii

Vices an

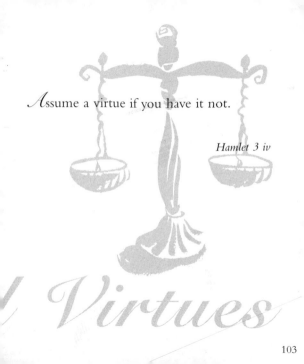

*A*ssume a virtue if you have it not.

Hamlet 3 iv

Virtues

What is a man,

If his chief good and market of his time

Be but to sleep and feed?

Hamlet 4 iv

Men of few words are the best men.

Henry the Fifth 3 ii

Suspicion always haunts the guilty mind;
the thief doth fear each bush an officer.

Henry the Sixth – Part Three 5 vi

Virtues

*H*eat not a furnace for your foe so hot

That it do singe yourself. We may outrun

By violent swiftness that which we run at,

And lose by over-running.

Henry the Eighth 1 i

Vices an

Men's evil manners live in brass: their virtues

We write in water.

Henry the Eighth 4 ii

The evil that men do lives after them,
The good is oft interred with their bones

Julius Caesar 3 ii

Vices an

$\mathcal{A}$nd oftentimes excusing of a fault doth
make the fault the worse by the excuse.

King John 4 ii

Virtues

*H*ow sharper than a serpent's tooth it is
To have a thankless child!

King Lear 1 iv

Vices a

The quality of mercy is not strain'd;
It droppeth as the gentle rain from heaven
Upon the place beneath. It is twice blest:
It blesseth him that gives and him that takes.

The Merchant of Venice 4 i

Virtues

*C*ondemn the fault and not the actor of it!

Measure for Measure 2 ii

*V*ices an

But man, proud man,

Dress'd in a little brief authority,

Most ignorant of what he's most assur'd,

His glassy essence, like an angry ape,

Plays such fantastic tricks before high
heaven

As makes the angels weep

Measure for Measure 2 ii

Virtues

*V*irtue is bold, and goodness never fearful.

Measure for Measure 3 i

Vices an

*R*eputation, reputation, reputation! O,
I have lost my reputation! I have lost the
immortal part of myself, and what remains
is bestial.

Othello 2 iii

Virtues

O, beware, my lord, of jealousy!

It is the green-eyed monster, which
   doth mock

The meat it feeds on.

Othello 3 iii

Vices an

Few love to hear the sins they love to act.

Pericles 1 i

Virtues

117

*A*ll places that the eye of heaven visits

Are to a wise man ports and happy havens.

Teach thy necessity to reason thus:

There is no virtue like necessity.

Richard the Second 1 iii

Vices an

*V*iolent delights have violent ends

Romeo and Juliet 2 vi

*T*empt not a desperate man.

Romeo and Juliet 5 iii

Virtues

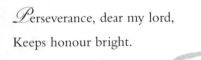

*P*erseverance, dear my lord,
Keeps honour bright.

Troilus and Cressida 3 iii

Vices an

$\mathcal{D}$ost thou think, because thou art virtuous,

there shall be no more cakes and ale?

Twelfth Night 2 ii

Virtues

In nature there's no blemish but the mind:
None can be call'd deform'd but the unkind.

Twelfth Night 3 iv

The
Passing
of Time

*T*hough age from folly could not give me freedom,

It does from childishness

Antony and Cleopatra 1 iii

And so, from hour to hour, we ripe
and ripe,
And then, from hour to hour, we rot
and rot;
And thereby hangs a tale

As You Like It 2 vii

$\mathcal{T}$ime is the old justice that examines all such offenders.

As You Like It 4 i

$\mathcal{T}he\ \mathcal{P}ass$

$\mathcal{D}$efer no time, delays have dangerous ends.

Henry the Sixth – Part One 3 ii

I care not; a man can die but once; we owe God a death.

Henry the Sixth – Part Two 3 ii

The Pass

*M*en must endure

Their going hence, even as their

 coming hither;

Ripeness is all.

King Lear 5 ii

The weight of this sad time we must obey,

Speak what we feel, not what we ought

to say.

The oldest have borne most; we that

are young

Shall never see so much, nor live so long.

King Lear 5 iii

With mirth and laughter let old
wrinkles come.

The Merchant of Venice 1 i

$\mathscr{B}$ut doth not the appetite alter? A man loves the meat in his youth that he cannot endure in his age.

Much Ado About Nothing 2 iii

Crabbed age and youth cannot live
  together:
Youth is full of pleasure, age is full of care.

The Passionate Pilgrim

g of Time

133

I wasted time, and now doth time waste

me

Richard the Second 5 v

The Passi

*F*ull fathom five thy father lies;

Of his bones are coral made;

Those are pearls that were his eyes:

Nothing of him that doth fade

But doth suffer a sea-change

Into something rich and strange.

The Tempest 1 ii

... *W*hat's past is prologue, what to come
In yours and my discharge.

The Tempest 2 i

$\mathcal{T}$ime hath, my lord, a wallet at his back,

Wherein he puts alms for oblivion,

A great-siz'd monster of ingratitudes.

Those scraps are good deeds past, which
   are devour'd

As fast as they are made, forgot as soon

As done.

Troilus and Cressida 3 iii

For beauty, wit,
High birth, vigour of bone, desert in
    service,
Love, friendship, charity, are subjects all
To envious and calumniating Time.
One touch of nature makes the whole
    world kin.

Troilus and Cressida 3 iii

Present mirth hath present laughter;
What's to come is still unsure.
In delay there lies no plenty,
Then come and kiss me, sweet and twenty
Youth's a stuff will not endure

Twelfth Night 2 iii

The whirligig of time brings in his revenges.

Twelfth Night 5 i

Sleep & Dreams

...*W*eariness

Can snore upon the flint, when resty sloth

Finds the down pillow hard.

Cymbeline 3 vi

Sleep and

O sleep, O gentle sleep,

Nature's soft nurse, how have I

   frightened thee,

That thou no more will weigh my

   eyelids down,

And steep my senses in forgetfulness?

Henry the Fourth – Part Two 3 i

Dreams

Sleep that knits up the ravel'd sleave of
    care,
The death of each day's life, sore labour's
    bath,
Balm of hurt minds, great nature's second
    course,
Chief nourisher in life's feast.

Macbeth 2 ii

Sleep and

*T*rue, I talk of dreams,

Which are the children of an idle brain,

Begot of nothing but vain fantasy

Romeo and Juliet 1 iv

Care keeps his watch in every old man's
  eye,
And where care lodges sleep will never lie;
But where unbruised youth with
  unstuff'd brain
Doth couch his limbs, there golden sleep
  doth reign.

Romeo and Juliet 2 iii

Sleep an

That, if then I had waked after a long sleep,

Will make me sleep again; and then, in

    dreaming,

The clouds me thought would open and

    show riches,

Ready to drop upon me; that, when I wak'd

I cried to dream again.

The Tempest 3 ii

Dreams

*W*e are such stuff

As dreams are made on; and our little life

Is rounded with a sleep.

The Tempest 4 i

Insults

Highly fed and lowly taught.

All's Well That Ends Well 2 ii

Pray you, stand farther from me.

Antony and Cleopatra 1 iii

The most infectious pestilence upon thee!

Antony and Cleopatra 2 v

*A*way, you cut-purse rascal! You filthy bung, away! … Away, you bottle-ale rascal!

Henry the Fourth – Part Two   2 iv

*P*eace, ye fat-guts!

Henry the Fourth – Part One   2 ii

Insults

*Y*ou starvelling, you eel-skin, you dried neat's-tongue, you bull's-pizzle, you stock fish – O for breath to utter what is like thee! – you tailor's-yard, you sheath, you bow-case, you vile standing tuck!

Henry the Fourth – Part One 2 iv

Insults

*Y*ou whoreson cullionly barbermonger

King Lear 2 ii

...*A*rt nothing but the composition of a
knave, beggar, coward, pander, and the son
and heir of a mongrel bitch

King Lear 2 ii

*T*hou whoreson zed! thou unnecessary
letter!

King Lear 2 ii

*W*hen he makes water his urine is
congeal'd ice.

Measure for Measure 3 ii

I dote on his very absence.

The Merchant of Venice 1 ii

*Y*ou juggler! You cankerblossom!

A Midsummer Night's Dream 3 ii

...*y*ou counterfeit, you puppet you!

A Midsummer Night's Dream 3 ii

*H*ow low am I, thou painted maypole?

A Midsummer Night's Dream 3 ii

Insults

*O*ut of my sight! Thou dost infect my eyes.

Richard the Third 1 ii

Thou art unfit for any place but hell.

Richard the Third 1 ii

A plague o' both your houses!

Romeo and Juliet 3 i

*O*ut, you green-sickness carrion! Out,

you baggage!

You tallow-face!

Romeo and Juliet 3 v

Insults

*Y*ou taught me language, and my profit
  on't
Is, I know how to curse.

The Tempest 1 ii

About William Shakespeare

William Shakespeare, recently voted man of the millennium, is regarded as the world's greatest playwright and poet. He was born in Stratford-Upon-Avon on April 23rd 1564 and died on April 23rd 1616. In his career as a successful and popular playwright he wrote 37 plays, 154 sonnets and a number of other poems. In spite of his claim in *The Sonnets* to be writing undying verse, Shakespeare took little care to publish and preserve his own work. *The Sonnets* appeared in a pirated edition in 1609, whilst his plays were only collected and published in 1623, seven years after his death.

Little is known of Shakespeare's life. He married Anne Hathaway in 1582 and had three children: Susanna, Judith and Hamnet. He moved to London in the mid-1580s and, in the following ten years, established himself as a leading playwright. In 1613, after his theatre, the Globe, had burned down, Shakespeare retired to Stratford-Upon-Avon.